WEATHER

WIND
AND US

Jillian Powell

Illustrated by Cilla Eurich

Smart Apple Media

First published in the UK in 1998 by
Belitha Press Limited
London House, Great Eastern Wharf,
Parkgate Road, London SW11 4NQ

Text by Jillian Powell   Illustrations by Cilla Eurich
Text and illustrations copyright © Belitha Press Ltd 1998
Cover design by The Design Lab

Published in the United States by
Smart Apple Media
123 South Broad Street
Mankato, Minnesota 56001

ISBN: 1-887068-41-4

Library of Congress Cataloging-in-Publication Data
Powell, Jillian.
    Wind and us / Jillian Powell : illustrated by Cilla Eurich.
      p.   cm. — (Weather)
    Includes index.
    Summary: Describes the wind, its effects on the weather and the
environment, and uses people make of the wind.
    ISBN (invalid) 1-887068-41-4
    1. Wind—Juvenile literature. 2. Weather—Juvenile literature.
[1. Wind.] I. Eurich, Cilla, ill. II. Title. III. Series: Powell,
Jillian. Weather.
QC931.4.P68 1998
551.51'8—dc21
                                                98-11198

Printed in Hong Kong

9   8   7   6   5   4   3   2   1

Picture acknowledgements
J.Allan Cash: 14, 16, 20, 28.
Eye Ubiquitous: 18 R.D. Raby.
Getty Images: front cover, 24 Randy Wells,
12, 22 Martin Puddy.
Robert Harding Picture Library: 8 Dr Muller.
Telegraph Colour Library: 4 A.Tilley,
10 Masterfile.
Zefa: 6 Kohlhas.

Contents

Words in **bold** are explained in the list
of useful words on pages 30 and 31.

What is the wind?

We can't see the wind, but we can feel it when it blows against our skin or ruffles our hair.

When it blows very hard, we can hear it making a whistling sound through windows and under doors.

WIND FACT

Warm air rises above cool air because it is lighter.

Wind makes
wet clothes dry by
shaking out drops
of water. Dampness
from our clothes
evaporates into
the air.

But what
is the wind?

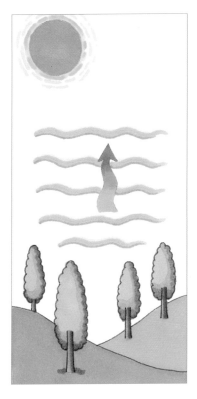

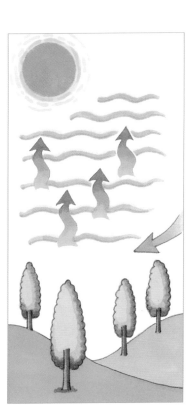

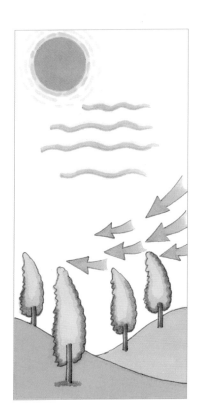

When land is
warmed by
the sun, the air
above it gets
warmer, too.

The warm air
rises and cooler
air blows in to
take its place.

The moving
air is wind.

Windy days

The wind makes clouds race across the sky. It makes **ripples** on water and in fields of tall grass or crops.

It blows trees about, making their leaves **rustle** and their branches creak.

WIND FACT

A gentle wind is called a breeze.

Sometimes it is hard to walk in a strong wind. Hats blow away and umbrellas turn inside out.

Flags flutter on a windy day.

The arrow on a **weather vane** spins around to show which way the wind is blowing.

A south wind blows from the south.

Wind power

Have you ever held a pinwheel? The wind makes it spin around and around.

8

People have always used the power of wind. Sailors used the wind to push their ships forward.

Windmills were used to grind grain and pump water out of wet land.

The wind turns the **sails** of the windmill, working the machinery inside.

Modern windmills, called wind turbines, are used to make electricity. They are linked together on wind farms.

Enjoying windy weather

Being outside on a windy day can excite us and fill us full of **energy**. We can fly a kite in an open space and watch how the wind sends it soaring and diving in the sky.

There are lots of other ways to enjoy windy weather.

WIND FACT

Kites were first flown in China about 2,500 years ago.

We can sail a boat across the
water as the wind fills its sails . . .

Windsurf across
the water on
a sailboard . . .

Fly in a hot-air balloon,
or watch as the wind carries
the balloon across the sky.

Hot-air balloons rise
because the heated air
inside them is lighter
than the air outside.
They can fly only when
the wind is gentle.

Winter and summer winds

Some winds are gentle; others are stronger. Winter winds can blow snow into a **blizzard**. Farm animals can be lost in deep snow.

Snowstorms make it difficult to see, so driving is dangerous. The wind can pile snow into deep **snowdrifts**.

WIND FACT

Wind that blows very hard can burn your skin.

12

The wind makes a cold day feel colder. We call this **wind chill**. Clothes keep out the wind and trap warm air around the body.

Summer breezes can cool things off on a hot sunny day. At the beach, people sometimes sit behind **wind breaks** if the breeze is strong.

Wind, plants, and animals

The wind spreads the seeds of plants and trees. The seeds are very light, so they can be carried a long way. The puffball mushroom puffs out clouds of **spores** when the wind blows against it.

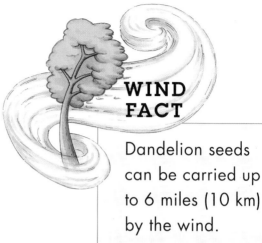

WIND FACT

Dandelion seeds can be carried up to 6 miles (10 km) by the wind.

Some seeds have wings that act like tiny helicopters. Others float like **parachutes**.

A bird's feathers help it glide in the wind. Steady winds help **migrating** birds fly thousands of miles.

15

Rabbits sniff the air while they are feeding. The wind can carry the **scent** of a **predator**, and warn the rabbits that danger is near.

Stormy winds

In stormy weather, the wind blows very hard and heavy rain falls. Trees can be blown down, crushing cars and blocking roads. **Power lines** can be broken, leaving homes without heat and light.

WIND FACT

The strongest wind in the world is called a **hurricane**.

16

Stormy winds can blow chimneys and roof tiles off of houses.

Tornadoes are the fastest winds in the world. They spin and swirl over land at more than 180 miles (300 km) per hour.

Gales blow the open sea into huge waves that can flood the land. Ferries and fishing boats have to stay in a **harbor** for protection.

Measuring the wind

Weather forecasters take information about the wind from **weather balloons**, and from ships and aircraft.

They use the information to make weather maps and **weather forecasts**. This instrument is an anemometer. The top spins around to show how fast the wind is blowing.

WIND FACT

Wind blows rain clouds around the world and brings our weather.

Satellites orbit around the earth and collect information about the weather. They send pictures back to earth.

On a weather map, this sign shows that the wind is blowing from the south at 10 miles (16 km) per hour.

Sailors, farmers, and aircraft pilots all use weather forecasts.

They need to know when the weather is going to be windy. **Windsocks** at airports and sea ports show which way and how fast the wind is blowing.

Staying safe in the wind

Tall buildings like skyscrapers are built from strong materials, such as concrete and steel, so they are not damaged when winds howl around them.

WIND FACT

Sometimes bridges have to be closed to traffic when the wind is very strong.

People build sea walls to keep the wind from blowing waves on to the land and causing floods.

Rows of trees and hedges keep winds from damaging crops and blowing the soil away.

Some animals stay safe in strong winds by hiding in underground burrows, or by huddling together.

Winds around the world

In some parts of the world, there are winds called monsoons. For part of the year they blow from the land.

Then they change direction and blow from the sea, bringing heavy rain. This city in India has been flooded by monsoon rains.

WIND FACT

Chinook means snow-eater in the Pacific Northwest.

Some winds have special names.

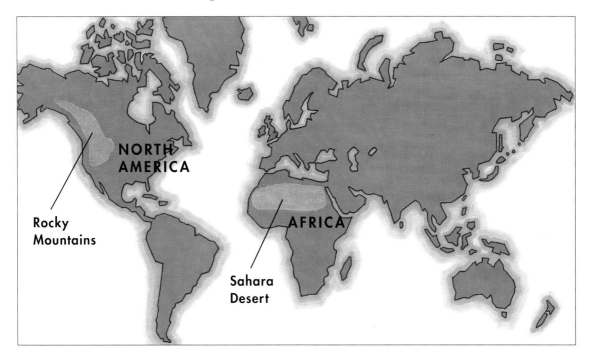

The chinook is a warm, dry wind that blows across the Rocky Mountains in North America. It can melt snow in a few hours.

The sirocco is a hot, dusty wind that blows off the Sahara **Desert** in North Africa.

Shaping the land

Wind can shape the way things look. In the **desert** it makes **ripples** in the sand, and blows it into high **dunes**.

WIND FACT

Wind changes the land more easily if there are no plants to protect it.

24

Plants found in very
windy places are short and
grow close to the earth.
They spread out their roots
and stay close together to
keep out of the wind.

Wind blows
rain or bits of
sand against
rocks. Over
a long time
this can **erode**
the rocks into
strange shapes.

When winds always blow
the same way, they can
make trees twist and
bend over as they grow.

25

Harmful winds

Fire and smoke are carried by the wind. After hot, dry weather strong breezes can spread forest fires by blowing sparks and flames through the dry wood.

WIND FACT

Wide forest paths help to stop fires from spreading.

Fumes from cars, factories, and power stations cause air **pollution**.

The pollution in the air turns clean rain into **acid rain**.

Acid rain kills trees and makes lakes poisonous. It also dissolves the stone on buildings.

The wind can blow pollution from one country to make acid rain in another country.

Wind worship

Strong winds can be powerful and dangerous. People have always been afraid of them.

People once believed the winds were gods and built **temples** to them. The Temple of the Winds in **Athens** was built about 2,000 years ago. When it was first built it had a **weather vane** on top, one of the first in the world.

WIND FACT

In Chinese **myths**, Mrs. Wind rode among the clouds on a tiger.

People believed
that if the wind gods
became angry they
would destroy houses,
crops, and ships at sea.

They also believed that
wind gods helped people
by blowing sailing ships
along and bringing flowers
in the spring.

Words to remember

acid rain Rain that carries dangerous pollution.

Athens The capital city of Greece.

blizzard A snowstorm where the wind blows the snow very hard.

desert A hot, dry place where there is little or no rain.

dune Sand piled into heaps by the wind.

energy Power to make things move. Energy gives us strength to do things.

erode To rub away, or erode.

fumes Poisonous smoke.

gale A very strong wind.

harbor Sheltered water where boats are kept.

hurricane A strong wind that spins around and around. A hurricane begins at sea.

migrating Traveling from one place to another.

myth A story made up to explain why things in the world are the way they are.

parachute A large piece of material that people use to help them fall slowly and safely from an airplane.

pollution Poisons made by people and machines that harm the earth.

power lines Wires that carry electricity to people's homes.

predator An animal that eats other animals.

ripples Small wave-like movements.

30

rustle A quiet sound, like the sound you make when you walk through dry leaves.

sails The arms of a windmill are called sails or vanes.

satellite A special spacecraft that travels around the earth. It collects information and sends it to computers on earth as numbers or photographs.

scent Another word for smell, often used about animals.

snowdrifts Snow piled up by the wind.

spores The seeds of some plants or mushrooms.

temple A place where people pray and worship.

tornado A strong wind that spins around and around. A tornado begins on land.

weather balloons Balloons carrying equipment that tell us about the weather.

weather forecast A prediction that tells us what the weather will be like in the future.

weather vane A machine that shows which way the wind is blowing.

wind break Anything that shelters people or plants from the wind.

wind chill When the wind makes the air colder.

windsock A piece of cloth shaped like a large sock that fills with wind and shows which way and how fast the wind is blowing. The foot end points away from the wind. The stronger the wind, the higher the end rises.

Index